Billionaires & Bodybuilders

The Road to Success is Equal

BILLIONAIRES & BODYBUILDERS: THE ROAD TO SUCCESS IS EQUAL

First edition. March 25, 2024.

ISBN: 979-8224879649

Written by Matt Weik and Marc Lobliner.

Table of Contents

Introduction

The journey to success is often a formidable and unpredictable path, filled with challenges, risks, and a burning desire to overcome them.

In this introductory chapter, we step onto the stage of "Billionaires & Bodybuilders: The Road to Success is Equal," a narrative that seeks to unravel the fascinating parallels between two seemingly disparate worlds, bodybuilding and business.

As we dive into the intricate fabric of these worlds, we will unearth the profound truths they share, beginning with a critical exploration of the role that risk plays in their paths to achievement.

The setting for our exploration has captivated countless individuals who have dared to dream, strive for excellence, and achieve success that appears unattainable to many.

Whether sculpting the perfect physique or building business empires, billionaires and bodybuilders embark on journeys fraught with uncertainty and potential pitfalls. The journey is one of risk, a fundamental concept that serves as the cornerstone of this narrative.

In our opening chapters, we introduce you to the curious notion that billionaires and bodybuilders are, in fact, more similar than they are different. While their physiques may seem lightyears apart, what it takes for them to win in their respective arenas is the same.

We present a bird' s-eye view of their worlds, offering a glimpse into the shared characteristics that define these two distinct communities of individuals. These ambitious pioneers understand that success is not easy and is equal but different.

With that understanding, they have mastered the art of risk-taking, perseverance, commitment, determination, and relentlessness.

We will explore the extraordinary courage and vision it takes to dream of achieving the seemingly unattainable. While the parallels between billionaires and bodybuilders may become apparent on the surface, deep down below the surface, they find common ground in the shared pursuit of their grand visions.

Through this visionary lens, we examine how billionaires and bodybuilders embark on life-altering journeys.

On one side, we have someone who wants to one day stand on the Olympia stage and take home the Sandow Trophy, while on the other, we have someone who is steadfast in their pursuit of adding three commas and nine zeros to their bank account.

We introduce the overarching theme of risk, intrinsic to their pursuits, with great significance. Risk is not just a word; it is the heartbeat of their stories. We set the stage for our exploration by emphasizing how embracing risk is a choice that can bring about both great success and colossal failure.

Risk is the bridge that connects the worlds of bodybuilding and business and is the backbone of this narrative.

As we journey through the chapters "Billionaires & Bodybuilders: The Road to Success is Equal," we invite you to embark on an odyssey of discovery, reflection, and inspiration.

Our first chapter provides the foundation for understanding the incredible, albeit challenging, paths that billionaires and bodybuilders tread in their relentless pursuit of success. The journey is complex, and the stakes are high, but as we shall come to appreciate, the road to success is equal.

We need to preface the start of our time together by saying we are not financial advisors, and we are not providing you with financial advice in this book. While we have been highly successful in both the fitness and bodybuilding industries and with entrepreneurship, this book combines our experiences, opinions, and data we've found during our journey that led us to compare billionaires and bodybuilders.

Whether you want to be a billionaire or bodybuilder one day, or neither at all, if you strive to be successful in any aspect of your life, the lessons and principles mentioned throughout this book will all apply. With that all being said, let's dive into the book together.

Chapter 1
The Power of Vision

A clear and compelling vision is a guiding star in pursuing success, illuminating the path forward.

This chapter will explore the significance of having a well-defined vision and goal. We'll unpack how billionaires and bodybuilders craft their visions for success and provide examples of successful individuals from both domains to illustrate the power of a strong vision.

The Importance of a Clear Vision and Goal

A vision is the cornerstone upon which the edifice of success is built. Without a clear and compelling vision, you may be adrift, lacking direction and purpose.

A vision serves as a beacon, guiding you toward your desired destination. It provides clarity and purpose, helping to navigate the complexities and challenges of the journey to success. One's efforts may become cohesive with a vision, and progress may be uncertain.

A well-defined goal is the tangible manifestation of a vision. It represents a specific and measurable objective that you work toward. A well-defined goal provides a sense of achievement and serves as a motivating force, driving you to take action and persist in the face of obstacles.

It's 100% necessary that short- and long-term goals must be set. Include a timeline for each that will push you to stay on track. These goals need to be not only attainable but measurable as well. Saying you want to be a billionaire in the next 90 days or to step on the Olympia stage next year while currently weighing 140 pounds is highly unlikely.

But write down your goals and put them somewhere you see them daily, such as your bathroom, refrigerator, desk, or anywhere else you frequent. Your short-term goals should all lead you to your long-term goal. Be sure to track and measure your progress to allow yourself time to evaluate your current situation and make the necessary changes if you fall short.

You need to track your progress to know if you're heading in the right direction. As a bodybuilder, you may see the number on the scale go up and think it's lean muscle mass when, in actuality, you're simply gaining body fat.

If you want to become a billionaire, you may have started your business and seen your monthly revenue grow. But it would help if you noticed that your expenses are increasing twice as fast, nullifying any profits you think you're making.

How Both Billionaires and Bodybuilders Create a Vision for Success

The process of creating a vision for success is a deeply personal and often iterative one. Both billionaires and bodybuilders craft their visions, drawing inspiration from their unique journeys.

Creating a Vision in Entrepreneurship

Entrepreneurs and aspiring billionaires create visions around business ventures and innovative ideas. These visions encompass financial goals and the impact they want to make on their industries and the world. The process involves strategic planning, defining business objectives, and visualizing the future state of their enterprises.

Visions in entrepreneurship are dynamic, adapting to market changes and the evolving needs of their target audience.

Any good entrepreneur will look at many people's problems and devise solutions. They fully understand that money follows attention and that if you chase money, all you'll do is find yourself out of breath.

When you solve problems and pain points that people have, you'll find people throwing money at you to help them. This can be through a service or a product. However, the key is understanding the problem and then reverse engineering how to solve it.

Creating a Vision in Bodybuilding

Bodybuilders often envision achieving an ideal physique and excelling in competitive events, such as the Mr. Olympia competition and the Super Bowl of bodybuilding.

Their visions are finely detailed and encompass muscle symmetry, size, and conditioning. The process begins with setting specific training and dietary goals, which, when combined, shape the vision. These visions are daily motivators, inspiring intense workouts, strict dietary plan adherence, and unwavering dedication.

As the vision takes form and their physique follows, it's a never-ending battle of improving weak areas of your physique and bringing up any lagging body parts.

In the movie *Pumping Iron*, Arnold Schwarzenegger had a perfect analogy when he said, "Good bodybuilders have the same mind when it comes to sculpting that a sculptor has. If you look in the mirror and need more deltoids and shoulders to get the proportions right... You exercise and put these deltoids on, whereas an artist would slap on some clay... that's the easier way. We go through the harder way."

It's about creating the vision first and then executing the plan you put in place.

The Goal Parallel

President Donald Trump is famous for saying he doesn't exercise because his body only has so much energy, which he dedicates to business, and exercise would deplete that.

Nonsense.

Science is precise that exercise does the exact opposite. It improves brain function, gives you more energy, and keeps you operating longer and better than your lazy counterparts.

The psychological implications of setting goals, achieving those goals, and then setting new, loftier goals carry over. Your brain sees it as one thing—success.

Success can be influenced by momentum. How can an NFL team go almost an entire game without scoring once, then come from behind and win 28-27?

Tom Brady fans know what I'm talking about.

Imagine having a hard workout in the morning, crushing it, and then going to the office with that winning momentum under your feet. Would you be more or less likely to close that deal or nail that presentation?

Exactly.

Winners win, and they keep winning. Winning in the gym leads to winning in life.

Examples of Successful Individuals from Both Domains

To underscore the power of a clear vision, we turn to examples of successful individuals from the worlds of entrepreneurship and bodybuilding who have harnessed the potency of their dreams to achieve greatness.

Elon Musk—The Visionary Entrepreneur and Innovator

Elon Musk, a prominent figure in the world of entrepreneurship, is a visionary whose ambitions know no bounds. His vision includes a future where humanity becomes a multi-planetary species, harnessing renewable energy and transforming the automotive industry.

Musk's vision has led to founding companies like SpaceX, Tesla, The Boring Company, and SolarCity, each contributing to realizing his overarching goal. He also took over the social media company Twitter, which changed the name to X to match his branding. His unwavering commitment to his vision has driven innovation and progress in various domains.

Arnold Schwarzenegger—The Visionary Bodybuilder and Actor

Arnold Schwarzenegger, a name synonymous with bodybuilding and Hollywood, is a prime example of the transformative power of vision.

From his early days in Austria, he envisioned himself becoming a world-class bodybuilder. His clear and compelling vision propelled him to win numerous bodybuilding championships, venture into acting, and eventually become the Governor of California. Arnold's vision extended beyond the gym, encompassing a multifaceted career and a lasting legacy.

In the following chapters, we will explore the lives of billionaires and bodybuilders, witnessing the transformative impact of a clear vision and how it catalyzes their journeys.

These visions are not mere dreams but a force that can propel you toward your goals. They inspire unwavering commitment, provide clarity in the face of adversity, and remind us of the extraordinary potential within all of us.

We encourage you to reflect on your vision for success and consider how it can guide your journey toward your aspirations.

How to Act Upon Your Vision

Here are some actionable steps you can take to act upon your vision:

1. Set Clear Goals: Define specific, measurable, and time-bound goals that align with your vision. These goals serve as milestones along your journey and help maintain focus.

2. Calculate Risks: Just as bodybuilders and entrepreneurs take calculated risks, assess the potential risks and rewards associated with your vision. Consider what you stand to gain and what you might need to sacrifice.

3. Plan Strategically: Develop a well-thought-out plan that outlines the steps and actions required to achieve your vision. Break down the plan into smaller, manageable tasks.

4. Stay Committed: Embrace unwavering commitment to your vision. Understand that success often involves overcoming challenges and setbacks, but persistence is the key to progress.

5. Embrace Discomfort: Be prepared to step outside your comfort zone. Growth and transformation occur when you embrace discomfort and take on new challenges.

6. Learn from Setbacks: View setbacks as opportunities for growth and learning. Analyze what went wrong, make necessary adjustments, and use setbacks as stepping stones to future success.

7. Seek Mentorship: Just as mentorship plays a crucial role for bodybuilders and entrepreneurs, bodybuilders and entrepreneurs should seek guidance and mentorship from experienced individuals who can provide insights and support.

8. Optimize Your Skills: Continue enhancing your skills and knowledge to align with your vision. Seek out opportunities for personal and professional development.

9. Balance Well-Being: Ensure that your pursuit of success doesn't compromise your health and overall well-being. Maintain a balance between your personal and professional life.

10. Give Back: As entrepreneurs contribute to their communities and philanthropic causes, consider how your vision can positively impact others. Find ways to give back and create a positive influence.

11. Stay Adaptable: Understand that your journey may require flexibility. Be open to adjusting your plan and approach based on changing circumstances and opportunities.

12. Celebrate Small Wins: Acknowledge and celebrate your achievements along the way. These moments of success serve as motivation to continue pushing forward.

13. Network and Collaborate: Connect with like-minded individuals who share your vision and collaborate with them to amplify your impact.

14. Visualize Success: Use the power of visualization to keep your vision vivid and motivational. Imagine yourself succeeding and achieving your goals.

15. Remain Resilient: In the face of challenges and naysayers, maintain your resilience and determination. Keep your vision at the forefront of your mind as a source of inspiration.

By taking these steps and embracing the mentality of risk-taking, commitment, and perseverance, you can actively work toward your vision, just as bodybuilders and entrepreneurs do.

Remember that success is a journey, and relentless pursuit of your vision will set you on the path to achieving your goals.

Chapter 1 Key Takeaways

- A clear and compelling vision is essential for success, guiding you toward your desired destination.

- A well-defined goal is the tangible manifestation of a vision, providing clarity, purpose, and motivation.

- Short- and long-term goals must be set, with a timeline for each, and they should be both attainable and measurable.

- Tracking progress is crucial to ensure that efforts are heading in the right direction and to make necessary adjustments.

- Creating a vision involves strategic planning, defining objectives, and visualizing the future state of endeavors.

- Solving problems and addressing pain points is crucial for entrepreneurs, emphasizing the importance of understanding the problem and devising solutions.

- Bodybuilders craft finely detailed visions focused on achieving ideal physiques and excelling in competitive events.

- Setting and achieving goals carries psychological implications, leading to a sense of success and momentum.

- Examples of successful individuals like Elon Musk and Arnold Schwarzenegger demonstrate the transformative power of clear visions.

- Actionable steps to act upon one's vision include setting clear goals, calculating risks, strategic planning, staying committed, embracing discomfort, learning from setbacks, seeking mentorship, optimizing skills, balancing well-being, giving back, staying adaptable, celebrating small wins, networking and collaborating, visualizing success, and remaining resilient.

- Success is a journey, and the relentless pursuit of your vision is crucial for achieving goals.

Chapter 2
The Road to Success Begins with a Decision

In the tapestry of success, every journey begins with a critical moment—the decision to embark on the path to greatness.

This chapter explores decision-making's pivotal role in pursuing success and how billionaires and bodybuilders make bold, life-altering choices to start their journeys. In these decisions, the fear of failure clashes with the courage to commit.

The Crucial Decision-Making Process

The journey to success is an intricate web of choices, each bearing its weight. The decision to act, to step out of one's comfort zone, and to confront the unknown marks the beginning of the journey.

One thing you need to wrap your arms around is the decision-making process, emphasizing its crucial nature in determining one's life's direction.

Decisions are not merely choices; they reflect one's values, priorities, and desires. Whether you pursue a specific goal in bodybuilding or venture into a new business, decisions can shape one's destiny.

By making decisions, one articulates one's aspirations and sets the stage for future endeavors.

Bold Choices to Start the Journey

The decision to pursue success is often bold and audacious. It requires the courage to break free from the shackles of mediocrity and take the first step toward something greater.

In bodybuilding, this choice might manifest as a commitment to a rigorous training regimen, a disciplined diet, or challenging competitions.

Entrepreneurs and aspiring billionaires may make decisions involving the launch of a startup, an investment in a groundbreaking idea, or pursuing an unconventional business venture. These initial, audacious choices often define their journeys' trajectory, setting them on a course filled with uncertainties and risks.

One question to ask yourself is, if you never took the step to act and commit, what would you have missed out on? The great Wayne Gretzky once said, "You miss 100% of the shots you don't take." Would you look back on your decision not to act with regret? Don't let fear hold you back—take that first step.

The Fear of Failure and the Courage to Commit

A common adversary that both billionaires and bodybuilders must confront is the fear of failure.

We all fear failure to some extent—it's only natural. The specter of potential setbacks and disappointments accompanies the decision to pursue success. It's in the face of this fear that true courage emerges.

Who cares if you don't make it the first time? Who cares if people doubt you and tell you it will never work?

It would help if you remembered that people who are doing better than you will never put you down. Only the people below will remind you of your failures to make themselves feel better for being average.

And if you're reading this book, you don't want to be average.

The fear of failure is a formidable obstacle that can paralyze you and deter you from venturing into the unknown. However, those who dare to commit and push forward stand the best chance of success despite the fear.

In the face of fear, courage is not the absence of doubt but the ability to act despite it. It is the determination to persist even when the odds seem insurmountable.

Billionaires and bodybuilders exhibit this tenacity as they commit to their goals, pushing past the anxieties and uncertainties inherent in their journeys to greatness.

Fail at the Gym, Not in Life

Every lifter has failed before their 8th rep. We've all hit that wall. But we work to overcome that failure and hit a new PR (personal record) in our next session. By failing and overcoming in the gym, we set the stage for us to overcome any shortcomings in life.

Did you miss that promotion? Work harder and get it next time.

A great baseball player will take thousands of swings weekly for 3-5 at-bats per game. They miss the balls in batting practice to hit the dingers in the game! Reps and reps and reps are what make great athletes great, and the process of practicing will make you better.

By overcoming failures in any part of your life, your brain will become accustomed to overcoming obstacles in ANY part of your life to succeed and achieve unlimited success.

Make Better Decisions Along Your Journey

Here's how you can make better decisions to set yourself up for success:

1. Define Your Vision and Goals: Clearly articulate your vision and specific goals. Having a well-defined destination is the foundation for making decisions that align with your vision.

2. Align Decisions with Your Vision: Whenever you face a decision, evaluate how it fits into your overarching vision. Consider whether the choice brings you closer to your goals or takes you further away.

3. Prioritize Goals: Not all goals are equally important. Prioritize your objectives to focus your decision-making on the most important goals.

4. Consider Long-Term Impact: Think about the long-term consequences of your decisions. Will they contribute to the sustainability and success of your vision over time?

5. Evaluate Risks and Rewards: Just as billionaires and bodybuilders assess risks, weigh the potential risks and rewards associated with each decision. Are you willing to take calculated risks to move closer to your vision?

6. Gather Information: Make informed decisions by gathering relevant information and insights. Consult experts, conduct research, and seek advice from mentors when needed.

7. Seek Diverse Perspectives: Consider different viewpoints and perspectives when making decisions. Diverse input can lead to more well-rounded choices.

8. Trust Your Instincts: Trust your intuition and instincts, especially when deciding. Gut feelings can be powerful allies in decision-making.

9. Stay Adaptable: Be open to adapting your decisions as circumstances change. Your vision may remain constant, but achieving it may require flexibility.

10. Avoid Impulsive Choices: Resist impulsive decisions that deviate from your vision. Take the time to reflect and evaluate the implications of your choices.

11. Learn from Past Decisions: Reflect on past decisions and their outcomes. Use this reflection to learn and improve future decision-making.

12. Take Ownership of Decisions: Take responsibility for your choices. Acknowledge successes and failures as steps toward achieving your vision.

13. Maintain Focus: Concentrate on the most critical decisions directly impacting your vision. Avoid minor choices that contribute little to your goals.

14. Monitor Progress: Regularly assess your progress toward your vision. Are your decisions leading to the desired results, or is adjustment required?

15. Celebrate Milestones: Celebrate the achievements and milestones that result from your well-informed decisions. Recognizing your progress can motivate and encourage you.

16. Embrace Trial and Error: Not all decisions will lead to immediate success. Be prepared to iterate and adjust as needed to refine your choices.

By following these principles and maintaining a clear vision and goal, you can make better decisions that align with your aspirations and ensure that you stay on the path to success, just as billionaires and bodybuilders do.

Your choices become the building blocks of your journey, shaping your future in line with your vision.

Chapter 2 Key Takeaways

- Every journey to success starts with a critical decision to embark on the path to greatness.

- The decision-making process is crucial, reflecting one's values, priorities, and desires, setting the stage for future endeavors.

- Bold choices to start the journey often require courage to break free from mediocrity and take the first step toward something greater.

- Confronting the fear of failure is essential for progress, as courage emerges from the determination to act despite doubts and uncertainties.

- Overcoming failures in the gym or in life builds resilience and fosters a mindset of continuous improvement and success.

- Strategies for making better decisions include defining vision and goals, aligning decisions with vision, prioritizing goals, considering long-term impact, evaluating risks and rewards, gathering information, seeking diverse perspectives, trusting instincts, staying adaptable, avoiding impulsive choices, learning from past decisions, taking ownership of decisions, maintaining focus, monitoring progress, celebrating milestones, and embracing trial and error.

Chapter 3
The Art of Taking Calculated Risks

Risk is the crucible in which the journey to success is forged, and the ability to take calculated risks is a fundamental skill that both billionaires and bodybuilders possess.

In this chapter, we will examine the intricate world of risk, analyze the different types of risks in bodybuilding and business, explore the role of risk assessment and mitigation strategies, and highlight the remarkable stories of individuals who have mastered the art of risk-taking.

Analyzing the Different Types of Risks

Pursuing success is not risk-free—quite the opposite. This chapter examines the diverse and often multifaceted nature of risks individuals encounter along their journeys. Whether in bodybuilding or business, risks come in various forms, each with challenges and potential rewards.

In the world of bodybuilding, physical risks are paramount. Engaging in intense training regimens, heavy lifting, and stringent dietary plans is risky. These actions can lead to injuries, overtraining, or long-term health issues. Bodybuilders must carefully navigate these physical risks to achieve their desired outcomes.

Conversely, financial risks, market uncertainties, and competition are the order of the day in business and entrepreneurship. Entrepreneurs must make calculated bets on their ventures, often risking substantial capital and personal resources. They must also face the risk of failure, which can be financially and emotionally taxing.

The Role of Risk Assessment and Mitigation Strategies

The art of taking calculated risks is not about plunging unthinkingly into the unknown; it's about making informed decisions. This section explores the critical role of risk assessment and mitigation strategies.

Both billionaires and bodybuilders employ methods to evaluate potential risks and develop plans to minimize their impact.

In bodybuilding, risk assessment may involve listening to one's body, tracking progress, and seeking professional guidance to avoid overtraining or injuries. Mitigation strategies include strategic rest periods, proper warm-up routines, and injury prevention techniques.

Entrepreneurs use market research, financial modeling, and expert advice to assess and mitigate potential risks. They create contingency plans, diversify their investments, and constantly adapt to changing market conditions. The ability to pivot and adjust is a core aspect of successful risk management.

A Billionaire and Bodybuilder Never Decide Their Fate

It would be nice to decide your fate. Unfortunately, that isn't the case in most circumstances. When it comes to entrepreneurs and bodybuilders, it's the market and judges that decide their ultimate fate.

It doesn't matter how hard you work, how much muscle you carry with low body fat, how much revenue you generate, how great your idea is, or how many hours you put into building your business or physique—success or failure lies in someone else's hands.

When you look at entrepreneurs, the market decides if your product or service is good. The market decides if they will pay how much you are charging. The market will either praise or scrutinize what you've produced.

You may think you have the best product or service on the planet, but if the market doesn't see the value, you're left with a project you've dumped time and money into that isn't going anywhere.

On the flip side, when you look at bodybuilders, the sport is one of the most subjective. You don't hit a ball to score runs, you don't put a ball through a hoop to gain points, and you don't run into an endzone to score a touchdown.

In bodybuilding, you stand before judges who score you against everyone you stand next to. You could be the best bodybuilder and one of the worst the following day, depending on who shows up at any given competition.

In both cases, you can work hard and perfect your final product before bringing it to the stage or market, only to have someone else or others tell you it's not worth the value you thought it had.

Can you imagine spending years building a business around a product or service, dumping time and money into something others didn't find the same value in?

Or even worse, can you imagine spending years building your physique, pushing your body to its limits in the gym, then dieting down for 16 weeks where you never once venture off your plan only to place dead last at a show you needed to win to get your pro card?

If you want to achieve greatness in any aspect of your life, you'll have to take risks—financial risk, humiliation, failure, wasting time and resources, the list goes on and on. But without risk, some of the best inventions, businesses, and physiques would never have been built.

Risk will cause many sleepless nights, questioning whether your actions are worth it.

You'll ask if your actions are worth potentially risking it all. But it all comes back to the question of "what if?" What if you never took that chance? What if you never pushed yourself? Would you look back with regret? Would you look back and wonder what would have happened if you stuck with it and took the risk? Can you live with that feeling for the rest of your life? Can you live with regret?

Real-Life Stories of Risk-Takers

The essence of risk-taking comes to life through the stories of those who have navigated these treacherous waters and emerged triumphant. This section features real-life accounts of individuals who embraced calculated risks and turned them into stepping stones toward success.

These stories serve as a source of inspiration. From bodybuilders who pushed their physical limits, knowing the potential dangers, to entrepreneurs who invested in unproven ideas and faced the possibility of financial ruin, they showcase the rewards of calculated risks and the importance of courage and determination in the face of uncertainty.

Let's look at other real-life stories of risk-takers who aren't named Arnold or Elon.

Richard Branson—The Maverick Entrepreneur

Richard Branson, the founder of the Virgin Group, is known for his risk-taking spirit and entrepreneurship. He began his journey with a vision to revolutionize the music industry, and he took a significant risk when he signed the punk rock band Sex Pistols to his record label.

Despite controversy and skepticism, this move catapulted Virgin Records to success and established Branson as an innovative entrepreneur.

Branson continued to push the boundaries, entering the airline industry with the founding of Virgin Atlantic. The airline was a game-changer, offering luxury service at competitive prices. This risky venture disrupted the industry and made Virgin Atlantic a global brand.

Additionally, Branson's foray into space travel with Virgin Galactic is a testament to his risk-taking nature. Developing commercial space travel was an ambitious and daring move, and while it faced challenges and setbacks, Branson's vision and commitment ultimately led to Virgin Galactic's success.

Dorian Yates—The Bodybuilder Who Took Training Risks

A renowned bodybuilder, Dorian Yates is a prime example of taking risks to succeed. He revolutionized bodybuilding by introducing high-intensity training, which challenged the traditional training methods of the time.

His risk-taking approach emphasized shorter, more intense workouts and less volume. Many were skeptical of this radical departure from convention, but Yates believed in the effectiveness of his approach.

Yates went on to win six Mr. Olympia titles, cementing his legacy as one of the greatest bodybuilders ever. His risk-taking attitude, which included defying conventional training wisdom, led to his unparalleled success in the sport.

Oprah Winfrey—The Media Mogul and Risk-Taker

Oprah Winfrey's journey from a local radio host to a global media mogul is a story of immense risk-taking. Her vision was to create a talk show that tackled real-life issues, and she faced adversity and skepticism in the male-dominated television industry.

Oprah's bold move came when she took ownership of "The Oprah Winfrey Show."

This risky endeavor allowed her to have creative control and ownership of her program, transforming her into a media powerhouse. Her willingness to take such a substantial risk in her career set her on a path to becoming one of the most influential figures in television and media.

Ronnie Coleman—Defying Limits in Bodybuilding

In bodybuilding, Big Ron stands out as one of the most celebrated bodybuilders in history. This is a testament to his relentless risk-taking and unparalleled perseverance. Gyms across the globe would hear, "Yeah, buddy! Lightweight!" any time Ronnie was in the building. His charismatic personality made everyone gravitate toward him.

Ronnie Coleman's vision was crystal clear from the outset: to be the best in bodybuilding. However, what set him apart was his fearless approach to achieving that vision.

As a police officer in Arlington, Texas, Coleman risked it all by pursuing a career in professional bodybuilding. The decision was daring, as he was in a profession that demanded physical fitness but was unrelated to bodybuilding.

Coleman's commitment to his vision knew no bounds. He took substantial risks by dedicating his life to bodybuilding, even when it meant financial instability and uncertainty. The leap from being a full-time police officer to pursuing bodybuilding as a profession was a monumental risk that defined his journey.

Ronnie's story is a remarkable example of how calculated risk-taking can lead to tremendous success.

Coleman's risk-taking endeavors began to pay off through relentless training and unparalleled determination. He adopted a bold and audacious approach to weightlifting, often pushing his body to the limits with intense workouts and massive weights. His unorthodox training style, which was unconventional at the time, set him apart from other bodybuilders and contributed to his extraordinary success.

Ronnie Coleman's relentless pursuit of his vision led him to the Mr. Olympia stage, the pinnacle of professional bodybuilding. He took the stage against formidable competition, defying conventional bodybuilding norms and showcasing a physique of unparalleled size, symmetry, and definition.

His eight consecutive victories at the Mr. Olympia competition solidified his status as one of the all-time greats in the sport.

After retiring from the sport of bodybuilding, Ronnie created his own Ronnie Coleman Signature Series line of supplements. The brand took off and, to this day, is still doing well with him as the face of the company.

Ronnie's vision was to take his name, phrases, and image and use them to springboard a new line of supplements in hopes that his fanbase would support his business endeavor. They did, and to this day, he has one of the very few supplement lines that were started by actual bodybuilders and have stood the test of time.

Coleman's journey underscores the idea that success often requires stepping into the unknown, taking calculated risks, and demonstrating unwavering commitment to one's vision. His daring approach to bodybuilding, relentless work ethic, and willingness to push the limits redefined the sport and made him an icon in bodybuilding.

Ronnie Coleman's story continues to inspire aspiring bodybuilders today. It illustrates the transformative power of vision, risk-taking, and unwavering determination. His legacy is a testament to the potential that lies within us when we dare to take risks that are aligned with our dreams.

These stories of Richard Branson, Dorian Yates, Oprah Winfrey, and Ronnie Coleman highlight the transformative power of calculated risk-taking.

Their visions and willingness to venture into uncharted territory have redefined industries and set them on the path to remarkable success.

Each of these journeys inspires aspiring entrepreneurs and bodybuilders, demonstrating that taking risks aligned with one's vision can lead to extraordinary achievements.

Take Better and More Calculated Risks

Taking better and more calculated risks is a fundamental aspect of the journey to success. Here are ways to enhance your risk-taking abilities:

1. Define Your Risk Tolerance: Assess your comfort with taking risks in various aspects of life to understand your personal risk tolerance.

2. Set Clear Goals: Establish specific, measurable goals that serve as a foundation for making calculated risks. Knowing what you aim to achieve provides direction.

3. Conduct Risk Analysis: Assess each decision's potential risks and rewards. Consider the best-case and worst-case scenarios.

4. Gather Information: Make informed decisions by collecting relevant data and insights. Research, consult experts, and learn from others' experiences.

5. Seek Diverse Perspectives: Encourage different viewpoints and gather feedback from diverse sources to ensure a well-rounded understanding of the risks involved.

6. Start Small: Begin with minor, manageable risks to build confidence and experience. Gradually increase the scale of your risks as your comfort level grows.

7. Set Limits: Establish boundaries and limits for your risk-taking. Knowing when to stop or change direction can prevent catastrophic outcomes.

8. Develop a Contingency Plan: Prepare for potential setbacks by creating a backup plan. Knowing how to respond to unexpected challenges can mitigate risks.

9. Use Risk Management Tools: Apply risk management techniques, such as risk assessment matrices and scenario analysis, to evaluate and mitigate potential risks.

10. Balance Risk and Reward: Weigh the potential rewards against the risks involved. Ensure that the potential benefits justify the level of risk you're taking.

11. Trust Your Intuition: Don't underestimate your gut feelings. When based on experience and knowledge, intuition can provide valuable guidance.

12. Learn from Mistakes: Embrace failures as opportunities for learning and growth. Reflect on past risks and their outcomes to make better decisions in the future.

13. Stay Informed: Continuously update your knowledge and skills to make more informed and calculated risk-taking decisions.

14. Collaborate and Seek Mentorship: Work with mentors and peers with risk management experience. Their guidance can help you make better decisions.

15. Evaluate the Impact on Your Vision: Consider whether a risk aligns with your overarching vision and goals. Ensure that taking the risk advances your mission.

16. Stay Adaptable: Be flexible and ready to adjust your risk-taking strategy in response to changing circumstances and new information.

Balancing risk and reward is an essential skill on the journey to success.

By employing these strategies, you can take better, more calculated risks that move you closer to your goals and aspirations while minimizing potential negative consequences.

Chapter 3 Key Takeaways

- Risk is inherent in the journey to success, and the ability to take calculated risks is vital for both billionaires and bodybuilders.

- Risks in bodybuilding include physical dangers like injuries or health issues, while business risks involve financial investments, market uncertainties, and competition.

- Risk assessment and mitigation strategies are essential for making informed decisions, including listening to one's body, tracking progress, market research, financial modeling, and creating contingency plans.

- Success often relies on taking risks despite the fear of failure, as external factors like judges or market reception ultimately determine outcomes.

- Real-life stories of risk-takers like Richard Branson, Dorian Yates, Oprah Winfrey, and Ronnie Coleman highlight the rewards of calculated risks and the importance of unwavering commitment to one's vision.

- Enhancing risk-taking abilities involves defining risk tolerance, setting clear goals, conducting risk analysis, gathering information, seeking diverse perspectives, starting small, setting limits, developing contingency plans, using risk management tools, balancing risk and reward, trusting intuition, learning from mistakes, staying informed, collaborating and seeking mentorship, evaluating impact on vision, and staying adaptable.

- By employing the strategies in this chapter, you can take better, more calculated risks aligned with your goals and aspirations, leading to success while minimizing potential negative consequences.

Chapter 4
The Pain and Suffering of Pursuit

Success is rarely a smooth and painless journey.

This chapter discusses bodybuilders' physical and emotional pain during rigorous training regimens and entrepreneurs' psychological and financial challenges in pursuing their dreams. It underscores the common thread of embracing discomfort in both their journeys.

Physical and Emotional Pain in Bodybuilding

Bodybuilding is a pursuit that demands dedication and the willingness to endure significant physical and emotional pain.

This section explores the physical pain of intensive training, including muscle soreness, injuries, and grueling workouts that push the human body to its limits.

Beyond the physical aspects, bodybuilders also face emotional pain, such as self-doubt, frustration, and the mental toll of relentlessly pushing themselves.

The journey to success in bodybuilding is not only about building muscle but also about building mental grit and resilience.

Psychological and Financial Challenges in Entrepreneurship

Entrepreneurs face a different set of challenges on their path to success. These include psychological challenges, including the fear of failure, uncertainty, and the stress of managing a business.

The psychological toll of entrepreneurship can be significant, affecting individuals' well-being and mental health.

Financial challenges are another facet of the entrepreneur's journey. Starting a business often requires significant financial investments and a willingness to take financial risks.

Entrepreneurs may face periods of financial instability, requiring them to navigate economic turbulence and make tough decisions.

Embracing Discomfort as a Common Thread

Embracing discomfort is a shared experience in both bodybuilding and entrepreneurship. It is the acknowledgment that growth and transformation often come from pushing beyond one's comfort zone.

In either scenario, you must understand that embracing discomfort is a common thread in either journey and the valuable lessons it imparts.

In bodybuilding, discomfort is a constant companion. Pushing through pain and discomfort grows muscles, increases strength, and improves endurance.

Bodybuilders understand that the journey to success is filled with moments of discomfort, and it is in those moments that actual progress is made.

Entrepreneurs, too, learn to thrive in discomfort. They embrace the uncertainty, take calculated risks, and navigate through the challenges of business ownership. Discomfort becomes a teacher, pushing them to innovate, adapt, and grow their enterprises.

Resilience in the Face of Naysayers

On the path to success, whether as a bodybuilder sculpting a chiseled physique or an entrepreneur shaping a thriving enterprise, one constant companion that risk-takers must learn to navigate is the chorus of naysayers.

Often fueled by misconceptions and stereotypes, these individuals quickly cast judgment and doubt. Yet, the resilience to overcome their skepticism sets the determined apart from the rest.

The Misconceptions About Bodybuilders

Bodybuilders, with their sculpted physiques and dedication to physical fitness, are often labeled with derogatory terms such as "meatheads" or told they are devoid of intellectual depth (or, to put it not in politically correct terminology, that bodybuilders are stupid).

These stereotypes are a classic example of how societal preconceptions can attempt to diminish the profound commitment that bodybuilders invest in their craft.

In the face of such criticism, successful bodybuilders like Arnold Schwarzenegger and Ronnie Coleman have demonstrated unwavering resolve. They understood that their pursuit extended far beyond the weights and the stage. They knew dedication, discipline, and mental toughness were the cornerstones of their success.

In essence, they defied the labels imposed on them and proved that the art of bodybuilding is not just about physicality but also a testament to one's mental strength.

Bodybuilders can become some of the best entrepreneurs due to how they handle themselves as a bodybuilder. The ability to overcome, track progress, pivot, manage time, and put the puzzle pieces together when they scramble all over the table sets them apart from so many. They are regimented, and that's precisely what entrepreneurs need to be successful.

Entrepreneurs and the Money Myth

Entrepreneurs, especially those who achieve substantial wealth, often face misconceptions that they are driven solely by the pursuit of money. Critics may argue that their focus on financial success eclipses their capacity to contribute positively to society.

Yet, this perspective overlooks entrepreneurs' vital role in job creation, innovation, and philanthropy.

Successful entrepreneurs are not just motivated by monetary gain; they are visionaries who aspire to bring about positive change. They create businesses that employ individuals, providing them with livelihoods and opportunities for personal growth.

Entrepreneurship, at its core, is a vehicle for innovation and job creation that goes beyond the pursuit of profit.

The misconception that entrepreneurs only love money and the old saying that "money doesn't buy happiness" must be buried.

For starters, I know that I buy things that make me happy, don't you? Why would you buy stuff you don't want or don't make you happy? Not only that, but money provides you with options. Options you would only have if you had money.

So, despite what people say about money, it's an integral part of our lives, whether you want to admit it or not. People who wish to complain about those who are wealthy tend to be people who never have enough money to understand the difference.

Furthermore, many entrepreneurs who have achieved financial success actively engage in philanthropic efforts, giving back to their communities and supporting charitable causes. These individuals understand that with great success comes the responsibility to impact the world positively.

Entrepreneurs are some of the most giving and charitable people on the planet. Most don't talk about it, so you never hear about it. They don't provide for the sake of gaining exposure. They do it because they want to give back and help others.

As we dive deeper into the journeys of bodybuilders and entrepreneurs in the following chapters, we will witness the profound lessons that arise from enduring pain and discomfort. These lessons are a testament to the strength of the human spirit, the power of resilience, and the unwavering commitment to achieving success. As we continue, we encourage you to reflect on the discomfort you have faced in your pursuits and how it has shaped your path to success.

Perhaps you're going through something painful, and you feel stuck suffering. You're not. It would help if you weathered the storm so that you could see the light shine through the clouds as the storm passes.

Cold Plunges

By now, you have seen Joe Rogan and others plunge into ice-cold water that would immediately tense and lock up muscles while simultaneously sending shivers down the spine of anyone who dared to challenge themselves.

Shockingly, Rogan and others do it as a daily ritual without a single complaint.

But soaking themselves in a cold plunge bath isn't for their bodies...

Data is apparent that cold plunges blunt hypertrophy, or muscle gains. But they do this for their MINDS, not their muscles.

By cold plunging, they force their bodies to be uncomfortable, and if you've ever done it, you know it's tough. This gets the body accustomed to doing hard things, making complex things in their everyday lives much easier.

This is what bodybuilding does for you. Lifting is hard. Lifting and enduring the "suck" makes everything else in life that much easier.

Unfortunately, most people will never challenge themselves in such a way because they don't like the feeling of being uncomfortable and doing hard things.

How to Endure the Ups and Downs

Enduring mental and physical pain and suffering on the path to success is a testament to one's determination and resilience. Here are ways to navigate and persevere through these challenges:

Dealing with Mental and Emotional Challenges

1. Develop Resilience: Cultivate mental toughness to bounce back from setbacks and adversities. Focus on building emotional resilience and coping skills.

2. Maintain a Growth Mindset: Embrace challenges as opportunities for growth. View failures as learning experiences that can propel you forward.

3. Seek Support: When facing mental and emotional challenges, don't hesitate to contact friends, family, or a therapist. Sharing your struggles can be cathartic.

4. Practice Mindfulness: Incorporate mindfulness techniques into your daily routine to manage stress, reduce anxiety, and stay present in the moment.

5. Set Realistic Expectations: Avoid setting unrealistic or overly ambitious goals that may lead to mental stress. Establish achievable milestones that are motivating rather than discouraging.

6. Stay Positive: Focus on your strengths, accomplishments, and progress to foster a positive mindset. A positive outlook can help you overcome mental hurdles.

7. Visualize Success: Use visualization exercises to see yourself achieving your goals. This mental rehearsal can boost motivation and self-confidence.

Dealing with Physical Challenges

1. Properly Fuel Your Body: Consume a balanced diet that supports your physical activities. Eating well can provide energy, reduce fatigue, and enhance recovery.

2. Rest and Recovery: Prioritize adequate rest and sleep. This allows your body to recover and rejuvenate, which is essential for sustaining physical effort.

3. Listen to Your Body: Listen to your body's signals and respond to pain or discomfort by adjusting your training or workload. When necessary, seek medical advice.

4. Work with Professionals: Consider consulting with coaches, trainers, or physical therapists to ensure that your physical activities to achieve success are safe and effective.

5. Build Gradually: Avoid pushing your body too hard too quickly. Trying to do too much when you're not used to the load you're putting on your body can cause injuries or health issues. Pace yourself.

6. Stay Hydrated. Proper hydration is crucial for physical and mental performance. Dehydration can crush your performance and leave you with mental fog.

7. Use Pain as Feedback: Learn to distinguish between productive discomfort and harmful pain. Push through discomfort that contributes to growth but stop when it risks injury.

Remember that pursuing success often involves both mental and physical challenges.

Your ability to persevere through pain and suffering is a testament to your commitment to your goals. Implementing these strategies can help you better navigate the hardships on your journey to success.

Chapter 4 Key Takeaways

- Success entails enduring physical and emotional pain, whether in bodybuilding or entrepreneurship, highlighting the necessity of embracing discomfort in the journey.

- Bodybuilders face physical pain from intense training and emotional challenges like self-doubt, while entrepreneurs encounter psychological obstacles such as fear of failure and financial stress.

- Both bodybuilders and entrepreneurs learn to thrive in discomfort, viewing it as a catalyst for growth, innovation, and resilience.

- Naysayers and societal misconceptions often challenge both bodybuilders and entrepreneurs, requiring resilience and determination to overcome.

- Successful bodybuilders and entrepreneurs defy stereotypes, demonstrating the importance of mental strength and vision in achieving success.

- Cold plunges and other discomfort-inducing activities train the mind to handle adversity, making challenges in daily life more manageable.

- Strategies for enduring mental and physical challenges include developing resilience, maintaining a growth mindset, seeking support, practicing mindfulness, setting realistic expectations, staying positive, visualizing success, properly fueling the body, prioritizing rest and recovery, listening to the body, working with professionals, building gradually, staying hydrated, and using pain as feedback.

- Persevering through pain and suffering is integral to the pursuit of success, reflecting one's determination and commitment to achieving goals.

Chapter 5
Commitment and Discipline

Commitment and discipline are the cornerstones that provide structure and unwavering determination.

This chapter illuminates the pivotal role of commitment and discipline in bodybuilding and business, exploring the relentless commitment required to stay the course and the discipline needed to remain on track. It also dives deeper into various techniques and practices to maintain focus and dedication.

The Unwavering Commitment Required

Commitment is the bedrock of success, serving as a testament to one's dedication to a goal or endeavor.

In this section, we explore the unwavering commitment required in bodybuilding and business, emphasizing the need for you to stay true to your aspirations even in the face of adversity.

Commitment means adhering to a strict training regimen, diet, and lifestyle in bodybuilding. It entails consistently pushing one's physical limits and refusing to give in to self-doubt.

Bodybuilders' commitment is evident in their sacrifices, such as adhering to a stringent diet and investing countless hours in the gym.

In business, unwavering commitment means persistently pursuing one's entrepreneurial vision, even when faced with setbacks and challenges. Entrepreneurs demonstrate commitment by dedicating themselves to their ventures and investing time, energy, and resources to bring their ideas to fruition.

Exploring the Discipline Needed to Stay on Track

Discipline is the compass that guides you toward your goals. Despite distractions, temptations, and obstacles, staying on track and maintaining consistent progress are required.

Discipline means adhering to a meticulously planned training program, dietary restrictions, and recovery routines in bodybuilding. It entails resisting the temptation to deviate from the path, even when faced with cravings or exhaustion. Discipline keeps bodybuilders focused on their ultimate goal and ensures that every action aligns with their vision.

Discipline involves creating and adhering to a structured business plan, maintaining a solid work ethic, and managing resources wisely. Entrepreneurs exhibit discipline by staying organized, setting priorities, and efficiently using their time and resources. Discipline enables them to navigate the complex world of entrepreneurship effectively.

Techniques and Practices to Maintain Focus and Dedication

Individuals often employ various techniques and practices to maintain high focus and dedication. Let's examine some strategies bodybuilders and entrepreneurs use to keep their commitment and discipline.

In bodybuilding, techniques like visualization, goal setting, and the support of a coach or training partner can help maintain focus and dedication. These practices ensure that every workout and meal serves a specific purpose in achieving the desired physique.

Staying focused and dedicated on your journey to success is vital for achieving your goals. Here are some techniques to help maintain focus and unwavering dedication:

1. **Set Clear Goals:** Define specific, measurable, and time-bound goals that provide a clear roadmap for your journey.

2. Prioritize Tasks: Identify and prioritize the most critical tasks that align with your goals and focus on completing them first.

3. Create a Routine: Establish a daily schedule with dedicated time for working toward your goals.

4. Break It Down: Divide your goals into smaller, manageable tasks to make them less overwhelming and more achievable.

5. Time Management: Use time management techniques like the Pomodoro Technique to stay productive and avoid distractions.

6. Eliminate Distractions: Identify and remove or minimize distractions in your environment, whether physical, digital, or mental.

7. Set Deadlines: Assign deadlines to your tasks and goals to create a sense of urgency and accountability.

8. Practice Mindfulness: Incorporate mindfulness and meditation to increase self-awareness and stay present in your work.

9. Visualize Success: Regularly visualize yourself achieving your goals and experiencing your desired success. This can boost motivation.

10. Maintain a Positive Mindset: Cultivate a positive attitude and focus on your strengths, achievements, and progress.

11. Stay Accountable: Share your goals with a trusted friend, mentor, or coach who can hold you accountable for your progress.

12. Celebrate Small Wins: Acknowledge and celebrate your achievements, no matter how small they may seem. Recognizing progress can boost motivation.

13. Stay Organized: Use tools like to-do lists, calendars, or project management apps to keep track of tasks and deadlines.

14. Stay Physically Active: Regular physical activity can help maintain focus, reduce stress, and boost overall well-being.

15. Seek Inspiration: Find inspiration in role models, success stories, or motivational content that resonates with your goals.

16. Take Breaks: Avoid burnout by scheduling regular breaks to refresh your mind and body.

17. Learn Continuously: Stay engaged and motivated and acquire new knowledge and skills related to your goals.

18. Surround Yourself with Positivity: Engage with supportive, positive individuals who encourage your journey.

19. Visualize the Consequences: Consider the impact of success and failure to motivate your dedication.

20. Review Progress: Periodically assess your progress, adjust your strategies if necessary, and celebrate your achievements.

Strategies such as time management, delegation, and setting clear objectives can help entrepreneurs maintain focus and dedication.

Additionally, seeking mentorship and continuously learning from experiences enables them to stay on track and achieve their goals, which nicely segues into our next chapter.

Chapter 5 Key Takeaways

- Foundational for success, commitment and discipline provide structure and determination in bodybuilding and business endeavors.

- In bodybuilding, commitment involves adhering to rigorous training regimens and dietary plans despite physical and mental challenges.

- In business, commitment means persistently pursuing entrepreneurial visions despite setbacks.

- Discipline guides people toward their goals, necessitating adherence to plans and resisting distractions.

- In bodybuilding, discipline involves following training programs and dietary restrictions, while in business, it entails strategic planning and resource management.

- Both bodybuilders and entrepreneurs employ strategies like goal setting, prioritization, routine creation, time management, and visualization to sustain focus and dedication.

- Techniques include setting clear goals, prioritizing tasks, establishing routines, breaking down goals into manageable steps, managing time effectively, eliminating distractions, practicing mindfulness, visualizing success, maintaining a positive mindset, staying accountable, celebrating achievements, staying organized, staying physically active, seeking inspiration, taking breaks, continuous learning, surrounding oneself with positivity, visualizing consequences, and reviewing progress.

Chapter 6
The Role of Mentorship

Mentorship is a powerful guiding force in the journey to success, offering wisdom, experience, and invaluable insights.

In this chapter, we will explore the profound significance of mentors in the journeys of billionaires and bodybuilders. We'll explore stories of mentorship and guidance and how mentors can play a pivotal role in helping you avoid costly mistakes along your path to achievement.

The Significance of Mentors in the Journeys

Mentors are seasoned navigators who light the way for those embarking on the treacherous voyage to success. We underscore their significance and how they act as beacons of wisdom, offering guidance and direction to those who seek to follow in their footsteps.

In bodybuilding, mentors are often experienced trainers or competitors who guide training techniques, nutrition, and competition preparation. They offer technical expertise and emotional support and help individuals navigate the sport's physical and psychological challenges.

In business, mentors are often successful entrepreneurs or industry leaders who offer insights into market dynamics, business strategy, marketing techniques, and leadership. They share their experiences, help individuals build valuable networks, and provide a sounding board for critical decisions.

How Mentors Help in Avoiding Costly Mistakes

Mentorship is not just about offering advice; it's about helping you avoid costly mistakes that could otherwise hinder your progress. Mentors are essential to help you along your way and act as a safety net, providing insights that prevent missteps and setbacks.

Mentors share their experiences, enabling you to learn from their mistakes without making the same errors themselves. This knowledge is invaluable in avoiding pitfalls and navigating the intricacies of their respective fields.

Mentors also provide a sounding board for critical decisions, offering alternative perspectives and guiding you to make well-informed choices. Their guidance helps mentees make more calculated and strategic decisions, minimizing the risk of costly mistakes.

A mentor is like a cheat code for a video game you can't seem to beat. When the mentor provides insight or advice, it can help you unlock that new level of your business or physique you have been striving for. Don't downplay the importance of having great mentors in your life. Lean on them when necessary.

Personal Stories of Mentorship and Guidance

Mentorship is not just a concept but a living force that shapes individuals' destinies. Mentors can significantly impact an individual's journey and help fast-track their success.

Many bodybuilders have found guidance and inspiration in the form of experienced trainers and peers who propelled them toward their goals. These stories reveal the transformative power of mentorship in the realm of bodybuilding.

In business, we'll explore the journeys of entrepreneurs who benefited from mentors' guidance. These entrepreneurs learned valuable lessons that helped them navigate complex challenges and avoid common pitfalls. These personal anecdotes illustrate the critical role that mentors play in the world of entrepreneurship.

Matt Weik's Personal Story About Mentorship

I remember February 5, 2016, vividly in my mind.

It was the last day I wanted to be employed by someone ever again. The fact that I was working with people who didn't understand the business, didn't understand supplements, didn't exercise, didn't care about the food they put in their mouths, and I was told what to do simply because they were "executives" didn't sit well with me.

I was one of the most passionate people the company ever had on their team regarding health, fitness, supplements, and bodybuilding. That Friday, I chose to be unemployable (only in a positive sense). It was the end of one journey and the beginning of another.

I was leaving my job at one of the biggest supplement brands in the world and heading down a path of what I considered uncertainty.

In the weeks leading up to February 5, 2016, I talked with my wife about how unhappy I was working at this company. While I loved my customers and accounts, I hated the people I worked for and what the company had become during my tenure there. I told my wife I wanted to start a business.

Little did I know that it would quickly turn into multiple companies in my entrepreneurship journey.

For those who don't know my backstory, I was always an athlete. You'd always find me training as if I would one day take my skills to the next level. That wasn't going to be part of my story.

I was a writer in the industry for many years and built quite a following. Naturally, starting a writing service business in the industry made sense. Weik Fitness was born. The company combined personal training, nutrition consulting, and writing all under one umbrella and has since expanded into even more services.

In my first year of business, I had made more money than my salary at the supplement company I left. But I wanted more. That's where speaking with different people and finding a mentor changed my game.

It just so happens that Jimmy Mentis became one of my best friends, and when I started my first business, he became my mentor (whether he knew it or not). I could talk to him about anything, and he seemed to have all the answers.

In the first couple of years, I would lean on him with some ideas and get his feedback on whether or not he felt it was a good idea or worth the time/investment.

With the right mentorship and hard work, I quickly reached six figures for my first business (Weik Fitness). Due to the demand for my business, companies outside the health, fitness, supplement, and bodybuilding industries wanted my help with their businesses.

This led me to start my second writing business. At the time, I couldn't figure out a name for the new company, so I started throwing ideas out to Jimmy. He thought only a few of them were good.

His recommendation was to think outside the box. Knowing me, he told me to get a little edgy. That's when the name "Writing Rebels" was created. I texted Jimmy, and he immediately replied, "You better trademark that name before I do." Thankfully, I was faster than him, and a few months later, I got my trademark approved.

From the lessons and insight gained from owning my first business and working with Jimmy, Writing Rebel's revenue exceeded six figures in its first year. From there, I went on to invest in other businesses and have grown my portfolio of companies to my name.

Now, I'm not telling you this to brag. I'm telling you this because someone else is the sharpest tool in the toolbox. One thing I am is the hardest worker in the room.

When producing content, I average over 1,200 articles (1,000+ words) per year. I only know people who make as many articles for clients per year as I do. And that's not even counting what I write for my businesses.

My point is that my path to success is the same as anyone else's. Whether you're a billionaire or a bodybuilder, the road to success is equal. It would help if you had the same mindset, consistency, and will to win, regardless of your journey.

Find yourself a mentor who not only talks the talk but walks the walk. Find someone with a track record of winning. And use your ears more than your mouth. Listen to what they have to say. When you least expect it, they'll hit you with a gem that instantly causes you to look for a pen and paper or your notepad in your phone to write it down.

If I can find success by walking the path, you can too.

Marc Lobliner's Personal Story About Mentorship

When I was 14 years old, I was at a crossroads. My mother was battling an addiction problem and was in and out of rehab, and my father was enduring countless strokes due to his diabetes.

I was on a path to nowhere. I was getting into fights, running the streets, and had no plan for my future. I thought my life was over before it even began.

We used to have weight training for football at 1:30 pm daily. I was a mediocre player—I sat on the bench my first year and played a bit on the JV team my sophomore year simply because we didn't have enough players for me not to.

I sucked and gave no effort—my disdain for my situation in life carried over to everything I did. I got horrible grades, didn't apply myself, and was unrecognizable from the man people know now with multiple businesses, nine Inc. 500/5000 awards, and a loving family. I was a thug.

Two men would stay after the weightlifting class and train at a level I had never witnessed before. When I happened to stay even 10 minutes after class, I would see them screaming at one another, grinding out forced reps. To me, they looked like modern-day gladiators.

One was a guy who was a year my elder, Leon Hatten. He was an Outside Linebacker with his sights set on a D1 scholarship. We didn't hang out or associate in school, but I knew who he was—he was a stud. I was a nobody. Leon was 6' tall, 220 lbs., with light black skin and a muscular and intimidating physique. At the time, he looked like a black Adonis to me.

The other was Coach Cornell Myles. He was 6'3" and probably 270 lbs., with a crooked smile and an aggressive, almost southern accent. He was a high school security guard and a linebacker coach. I might misremember this, but I recall him repping 405 lbs. on bench press!

One day, I realized that if I was ever going to get out of my situation, football was my ticket, and I knew that getting big and strong was the only way. I decided to ask these two goliaths if I could train with them.

I mustered up the courage to ask them. At 2:30 pm, after the class, I walked over as they were getting prepped to crush the incline bench press. I asked them if I could train with them, and they replied with my worst fear: laughter.

I was mortified.

Coach Myles said, "If you can hang with us on incline, you're in."

I agreed, and with that, the workout began. By the grace of God Himself, I hung. I lifted like I had never lifted, lifting so hard that I couldn't move my arms the next day.

That day, my life changed. I had a reason to live.

Coach Myles and Leon might not even know this, but they mentored me along the way with life lessons that made me the success story I am today. They taught me:

1. **Meritocracy**: Work hard, and good things happen—I gained 70 lbs. in three months!
2. **Respect**: We were always on time and helped one another.
3. **Loyalty**: We were loyal to a fault, where I would have taken a bullet for these men and will to this day.

I learned so much more, but do you see the parallels? Everything they taught me is the EXACT lessons we have been preaching in this book.

It wasn't college or a self-help seminar that made me who I am today. Two strong men took me under their wing and mentored me. They thought it was just football training, but it was so much more.

Never be afraid to ask for help!

Chapter 6 Key Takeaways

- Mentors provide wisdom, experience, and guidance crucial for success in both bodybuilding and business.

- They act as beacons of wisdom, offering technical expertise, emotional support, and direction.

- Mentors can help you learn from their mistakes, preventing you from repeating errors and navigating challenges effectively.

- They offer insights, alternative perspectives, and guidance, enabling mentees to make well-informed decisions and minimize risks.

- Matt Weik's journey illustrates the transformative power of mentorship, leading to business success and growth through guidance and feedback.

- Marc Lobliner's story showcases how mentorship from Coach Myles and Leon Hatten transformed his life, teaching valuable lessons in meritocracy, respect, and loyalty.

Chapter 7
Overcoming Setbacks and Failures

Setbacks and failures are not the end of the road to success; they are the stepping stones to growth and achievement.

In this chapter, we will explore the art of overcoming setbacks and failures, analyzing the adversities faced by billionaires and bodybuilders. We will explore their strategies for bouncing back and learning from their mistakes and witness the remarkable resilience and determination that ultimately lead to success.

Analyzing the Setbacks and Failures Faced by Both Groups

Success is often a journey filled with large potholes and roadblocks, and both billionaires and bodybuilders are no strangers to setbacks and failures. We must examine your challenges and obstacles, including injuries, financial losses, market failures, and personal setbacks.

For bodybuilders, setbacks may include injuries, plateaus in training progress, or disappointing competition results. They can also result from choosing foods that cause bloating and blur muscle definition. These challenges can be emotionally and physically taxing, testing commitment and mental resilience.

Entrepreneurs and aspiring billionaires may face business failures, financial crises, or unexpected market downturns. These setbacks can be financially devastating and emotionally draining, challenging their resolve and belief in their goals. But you need to overcome these obstacles and learn from your mistakes.

Strategies for Bouncing Back and Learning from Mistakes

The ability to rebound from setbacks and failures is a hallmark of true success. To do this, you should look for strategies employed by billionaires and bodybuilders to recover from missteps and extract valuable lessons from their mistakes.

Learning from others' mistakes is much easier than making the same ones yourself.

In bodybuilding, strategies for bouncing back may involve adjusting training routines, seeking physical therapy, or reassessing diet plans and the food you put into your body. These experiences often lead to increased resilience, growth, and improved performance.

Entrepreneurs and business leaders often reevaluate business models, pivot, or seek mentorship (as mentioned in the previous chapter) to recover from setbacks. They learn from their mistakes, adapt their strategies, become more resilient, and better equipped to face future challenges.

The Resilience and Determination That Lead to Eventual Success

Setbacks and failures are not endpoints but rather stepping stones on the path to success. It would help if you strived for remarkable resilience and determination that drive both billionaires and bodybuilders to persist in adversity.

Bodybuilders demonstrate unwavering determination by pushing through injuries and plateaus, continually striving for progress. These challenges do not deter them but inspire them to work and train harder, be more intelligent, and have extraordinary tenacity.

Entrepreneurs exhibit remarkable resilience by learning from their business failures, refining their strategies, and continuing to pursue their goals. They recognize that success often requires navigating turbulent waters, and their determination remains undeterred.

No matter what you do, it would help if you were resilient and determined to accomplish something unique and leave your mark on this planet.

Overcome the Things That Push Your Way from Your Path to Greatness

Overcoming setbacks and failures is an integral part of the journey to success. Here are ways to navigate and bounce back from challenges:

1. Accept failure as a Learning Opportunity: View setbacks as valuable lessons that provide insights and opportunities for growth.

2. Stay Resilient: Cultivate resilience by developing mental strength and the ability to bounce back from adversity.

3. Analyze the Cause: Identify the root causes of the setback to prevent similar issues from arising in the future.

4. Refine Your Strategy: Adapt and adjust your approach based on what you've learned from the setback.

5. Seek Feedback: Gather feedback from mentors, peers, or experts to gain external perspectives and insights.

6. Reframe Your Mindset: Shift your mindset from a fear of failure to a focus on continuous improvement and progress.

7. Stay Positive: Maintain a positive outlook by focusing on your strengths, previous successes, and the potential for future achievements.

8. Set New Goals: Reevaluate and update your goals based on the lessons learned from setbacks.

9. Stay Persistent: Continue working towards your goals with unwavering determination and persistence.

10. Visualize Success: Regularly visualize your future success and the path to achieving your goals.

11. Manage Stress: Implement stress management techniques to cope with anxiety and stress caused by setbacks.

12. Network and Seek Support: Connect with mentors, peers, or support groups who can provide guidance and encouragement during challenging times.

13. Practice Self-Compassion: Be kind and compassionate to yourself, recognizing that setbacks are a normal part of any journey.

14. Focus on Solutions: Concentrate on finding solutions to overcome challenges rather than dwelling on the problems.

15. Maintain Adaptability: Embrace adaptability and flexibility to navigate changing circumstances and challenges.

16. Celebrate Small Wins: Acknowledge and celebrate minor achievements and milestones to maintain motivation.

17. Maintain Perspective: Put setbacks into perspective by considering the long-term trajectory of your journey.

18. Stay Goal-Oriented: Realign your focus on your goals to rekindle your motivation and sense of direction.

19. Stay Consistent: Stay consistent in your efforts and daily actions, even when facing difficulties.

20. Avoid Self-Blame: Avoid blaming yourself excessively for the setback, recognizing that external factors can play a role.

Remember that setbacks and failures are not indicators of overall success or failure but rather part of the journey to success.

By implementing these strategies, you can navigate challenges and emerge from setbacks stronger and better equipped for future endeavors.

Chapter 7 Key Takeaways

- Both billionaires and bodybuilders encounter setbacks such as injuries, financial crises, and personal setbacks.

- These challenges test commitment, resilience, and mental toughness.

- Bodybuilders adjust training routines, seek physical therapy, and reassess diet plans to recover from setbacks.

- Entrepreneurs reevaluate business models, pivot, seek mentorship, and adapt strategies to overcome setbacks.

- Bodybuilders demonstrate determination by pushing through injuries, striving for progress, and maintaining extraordinary tenacity.

- Entrepreneurs exhibit resilience by learning from failures, refining strategies, and persisting in the face of adversity.

- Accept failure as a learning opportunity and stay resilient.

- Analyze the root causes, refine strategies, and seek feedback.

- Reframe your mindset, set new goals, and visualize success.

- Manage stress, seek support, and maintain adaptability.

- Celebrate small wins, stay goal-oriented, and avoid excessive self-blame.

Chapter 8
Achieving Peak Performance

Reaching peak performance is the zenith of one's journey and the key to success in whatever you do or want to accomplish.

Both billionaires and bodybuilders achieve peak performance, exploring the optimization of their physical and mental capabilities. It unveils the unceasing quest for excellence and continuous improvement that defines their paths to success.

How Billionaires and Bodybuilders Reach Their Peak Performance

The attainment of peak performance is the ultimate goal for billionaires and bodybuilders, marking the culmination of their endeavors. It's the journey that leads them to this summit, highlighting the methods and approaches they employ to reach the pinnacle of their abilities.

Bodybuilders embark on a rigorous and systematic training regimen tailored to their goals. This training involves progressive overload, periodization, and meticulous attention to nutrition and recovery protocols. They continuously refine their approach, fine-tuning their routines to maximize muscle growth and strength.

On the other hand, billionaires seek to optimize their businesses, products, and leadership skills. They engage in strategic planning, innovation, and effective management practices.

Pursuing peak performance often involves adapting to market changes, identifying new opportunities, and cultivating a high-performing team.

The Optimization of Physical and Mental Capabilities

Peak performance is a physical achievement and a harmonious optimization of physical and mental capabilities. To achieve great success, billionaires and bodybuilders enhance their physical strength and endurance while fine-tuning their mental acumen.

Billionaires focus on optimizing their mental and physical capabilities. They prioritize personal well-being, practice stress management, and maintain a healthy work-life balance. Mental fortitude, leadership skills, and adaptability are critical to their success, enabling them to navigate complex business landscapes.

In bodybuilding, physical optimization involves nutrition, recovery, and fine-tuning training routines. This process also includes managing stress, sleep, and other lifestyle factors to ensure the body functions at its peak. Mental optimization is equally vital, with strategies like visualization, goal-setting, and mental resilience training to stay focused and driven.

The Quest for Excellence and Continuous Improvement

Average people are okay with the status quo. They are fine with the way things are and are opposed to change. In a sense, they are comfortable. But nothing great comes with comfort. To be great at anything, you need to be comfortable being uncomfortable.

Reaching peak performance is not a destination but a journey marked by the quest for excellence and continuous improvement. The unwavering commitment to progress defines the paths of both billionaires and bodybuilders.

For bodybuilders, the quest for excellence is a relentless pursuit of muscle growth, strength, and symmetry. They constantly seek innovative training techniques and nutritional strategies to enhance their physique and look at supplements to help fast-track their progress and results.

Progress is measured in increments, with each workout and meal contributing to the pursuit of excellence. It's a focus and culmination of things that bring the big picture together.

Billionaires share a similar quest for excellence in their businesses. They continuously strive to improve their products and services, streamline operations, and innovate. The pursuit of excellence is ingrained in their culture, focusing on delivering exceptional value to their customers and stakeholders.

Entrepreneurs aren't happy with the current version of anything they produce. They are always looking for ways to make it better for the end user or consumer. They push the boundaries of what is possible and look to turn the impossible into a reality.

Achieve and Maintain Your Peak Performance and Flow

Achieving and maintaining peak performance while maintaining a state of flow on the path to success requires a combination of mental and physical strategies.

Here are ways to help you reach and sustain your best performance:

Achieving Peak Performance

1. Set Specific Goals: Define clear, measurable, and achievable goals that give you direction and motivation.

2. Prioritize Tasks: Focus on the most critical tasks that align with your goals and tackle them with total concentration.

3. Create a Routine: Establish a structured daily routine with dedicated time for your most important activities.

4. Visualize Success: Use visualization techniques to see yourself succeeding and achieving your goals. This can boost motivation and self-confidence.

5. Practice Mindfulness: Incorporate mindfulness to stay present, reduce stress, and enhance mental clarity.

6. Embrace Challenges: Welcome challenges as opportunities for growth and improvement rather than obstacles.

7. Manage Stress: Implement stress management techniques, such as deep breathing or meditation, to stay calm and focused.

8. Maintain a Healthy Lifestyle: To optimize your physical and mental capabilities, prioritize nutrition, exercise, and adequate sleep.

Maintaining Flow State

1. Create a Distraction-Free Environment: Minimize distractions in your workspace to engage in your tasks entirely.

2. Set Clear Goals: Have a well-defined purpose and objectives for your activities to facilitate flow.

3. Challenge and Skill Balance: Aim for challenging tasks within your skill range to maintain a state of flow.

4. Eliminate Interruptions: Turn off notifications, avoid multitasking, and allocate uninterrupted time for focused work.

5. Get Feedback: Regular feedback can help you stay engaged and continuously refine your performance.

6. Immerse Yourself: Fully immerse in your activities and avoid overthinking or self-doubt.

7. Find Passion in Your Work: Seek tasks that genuinely interest and inspire you, making it easier to enter a state of flow.

8. Sustain Concentration: Maintain deep concentration and remain in the present moment, losing track of time.

9. Embrace Risk: Don't fear taking calculated risks to challenge yourself and sustain a flow state.

10. Stay Committed: Commit to your work, persist through difficulties, and stay motivated in your pursuit of success.

11. Track Your Progress: Monitor and acknowledge your achievements, which can boost your self-esteem and maintain motivation.

12. Celebrate Small Wins: Celebrate even the most minor successes, reinforcing your positive outlook.

Combining these strategies can help you reach peak performance, experience a state of flow, and stay on the path to success.

The key is to balance challenge and skill while staying focused and motivated.

Chapter 8 Key Takeaways

- Bodybuilders follow rigorous training regimens with attention to progressive overload, periodization, and nutrition.

- Billionaires optimize their businesses, products, and leadership skills through strategic planning, innovation, and effective management practices.

- Both groups prioritize personal well-being, stress management, and maintaining a healthy work-life balance.

- Mental fortitude, leadership skills, and adaptability are crucial for navigating challenges and achieving success.

- Both bodybuilders and billionaires pursue continuous improvement and excellence in their respective fields.

- Bodybuilders seek muscle growth, strength, and symmetry through innovative training techniques and nutritional strategies.

- Billionaires continuously improve products, streamline operations, and focus on delivering exceptional value to customers and stakeholders.

- Set specific goals, prioritize tasks, and establish a routine to maintain focus and motivation.

- Visualize success, practice mindfulness, and embrace challenges as opportunities for growth.

- Manage stress, maintain a healthy lifestyle, and optimize physical and mental capabilities.

- Create a distraction-free environment, set clear goals, and balance challenge and skill to sustain flow.

- Eliminate interruptions, seek feedback, and immerse yourself fully in tasks.

- Find passion in your work, sustain concentration, and embrace risk to challenge yourself.

- Stay committed, track progress, and celebrate small wins to maintain motivation and a positive outlook.

Chapter 9
Success is Equal but Different

In the tapestry of life, success is a multifaceted gem, and it takes different forms for billionaires and bodybuilders.

This chapter reflects on the intriguing interplay of similarities and differences in their paths to success. We explore how they define their versions of success and navigate the delicate balance between wealth and well-being.

Reflecting on the Similarities and Differences in the Paths to Success

Success is the common thread that weaves its way through the journeys of billionaires and bodybuilders, yet the paths they tread are distinct and unique. Throughout this section, we will take a step back and reflect on the parallels and disparities that define their pursuits.

Both billionaires and bodybuilders are relentlessly committed to their goals and endure physical and emotional challenges. Their commonality lies in their unwavering dedication, resilience, and pursuit of excellence.

The differences, however, are equally striking. Bodybuilders channel their efforts into sculpting their bodies, while billionaires invest in entrepreneurship and innovation. The contrasting domains reveal the diversity of success and the many avenues leading to it.

How Billionaires and Bodybuilders Define Their Versions of Success

Success is a deeply personal concept, and individuals in both groups define it on their own terms. Both billionaires and bodybuilders need to establish their unique visions of success. They could share similarities or be on polar opposite sides.

For bodybuilders, success is often defined by achieving peak physical condition, winning competitions, or overcoming personal fitness goals. Their success is measured in the sculpted muscles, strength, and endurance they attain. While they get on stage to be the best version of themselves, they strive to be the best on that day and win the show.

That said, even if they don't win the show, many bodybuilders look at their progress and consider it a success if they bring up lagging body parts or weak areas of their physique or conditioning, even if they lose to better competitors.

On the other hand, billionaires often associate success with financial prosperity, innovative business ventures, and making a meaningful impact on society. Their vision of success extends beyond personal achievement to include the broader impact of their endeavors.

Entrepreneurs don't all look at the financial side of the equation. Sure, most of the time, attention creates the flow of revenue, but it's the impact on their product or service that entrepreneurs truly strive to attain.

If their product or service can help at least one person, in their eyes, what they've accomplished is a success. It's all about solving problems for people.

The Balance Between Wealth and Well-Being

Balancing wealth and well-being is a delicate art that both billionaires and bodybuilders master on their journeys to success.

In their quest for financial success, billionaires often face the challenge of balancing wealth and personal well-being. Many realize that achieving their goals should not compromise their health, relationships, or overall quality of life.

Bodybuilders prioritize their well-being through physical fitness and health. They recognize the importance of maintaining a balanced and holistic approach to success and understand that true success includes a robust and healthy body.

Unfortunately, in their quest for success, far too many people double down on their work, minimizing sleep, healthy eating, time with family and friends, and mental health. They burn the candle at both ends until they work and push themselves into illness due to the drain on their bodies and immune systems.

When on your journey, it can be easy to immerse yourself in work and feel you need to keep pushing forward. There's nothing wrong with that. However, there is a time and a place for everything.

Just like there is a time to lock yourself in the office or weight room and get the job done, there's a time to let yourself out into the fresh air to refresh and rejuvenate your mental and physical energy.

Be sure to fuel your body with healthy foods and adequate amounts of water, and strive for a minimum of seven hours of sleep each night to allow yourself to recover from the previous day.

If you feel yourself seeping into a dark place, you're pushing a little too hard and must pull back slightly to regroup your focus and energy.

Your health needs to be a primary focus because if you lose it, you are unsuitable for your business, employees, or family. If you're striving for success, far too many say they'll "die trying." But what's the point of taking it to that extent if you never get to fulfill your journey because you didn't take care of yourself?

Entrepreneurs will work off of an hour or two of sleep each night. That's a terrible way to live. They need to realize that if they die, so does their business. All of that work was then for nothing.

In the case of a bodybuilder, why would you want to spend years building an impressive physique only to stop paying attention to your health and lose it, causing you to give up on your dream?

It's simply not worth it. You need balance in your life if you want to be successful.

Health is wealth. Once you lose your health, no amount of money can restore you to a clean bill of health. You now need to live with, deal with, and overcome any health issues that may arise due to poor lifestyle choices and decisions.

Don't allow that to be you.

Chapter 9 Key Takeaways

- Both billionaires and bodybuilders exhibit unwavering dedication, resilience, and pursuit of excellence.

- Bodybuilders focus on sculpting their bodies, while billionaires invest in entrepreneurship and innovation.

- Bodybuilders define success by achieving peak physical condition, winning competitions, and overcoming personal fitness goals.

- Billionaires associate success with financial prosperity, innovative business ventures, and making a meaningful impact on society.

- Balancing wealth and well-being is crucial for both billionaires and bodybuilders.

- Billionaires prioritize maintaining personal well-being alongside financial success to avoid compromising health, relationships, or overall quality of life.

- Bodybuilders understand the importance of a balanced approach to success, prioritizing physical fitness and health to achieve their goals.

- Entrepreneurs often neglect sleep, healthy eating, and mental health in their pursuit of success, risking burnout and illness.

- Prioritizing health is essential, as neglecting it can jeopardize one's ability to pursue and enjoy success in the long term.

- Balance in life is crucial for sustainable success, as health is wealth, and no amount of money can replace lost well-being.

Chapter 10

Lessons from Billionaires and Bodybuilders

We have been on a journey to examine billionaires and bodybuilders, exploring their arduous yet rewarding paths to success.

The time has come to distill the essence of their experiences into meaningful lessons, provide actionable advice for you to apply in your own lives, and inspire and motivate you to pursue your dreams.

As mentioned at the beginning of this book, billionaires and bodybuilders are used throughout due to their perceived differences. Billionaires are presumed to be highly intelligent and bodybuilders to be, well... not.

After reading this book, you'll realize that the comments you typically hear about bodybuilders aren't accurate and that bodybuilders can make some of the best entrepreneurs due to their mentality and ability to persevere and overcome any obstacle.

That said, it doesn't matter what your goal is or how you envision your image of success; you can apply the lessons learned from both groups to your life.

Summarizing the Key Takeaways from the Book

We've discovered that success is a complex tapestry woven with a common thread of determination, resilience, and unwavering commitment. Let's examine and reflect on the key takeaways from our exploration of the lives of billionaires and bodybuilders.

1. The Power of Commitment: Commitment is the cornerstone of any successful journey. Both billionaires and bodybuilders exhibit unyielding dedication to their goals, and it is through their commitment that they overcome challenges and achieve their dreams.

2. Embracing Discomfort: Success often lies just beyond one's comfort zone. Billionaires and bodybuilders have mastered the art of embracing discomfort and understanding that growth and transformation occur when we push ourselves beyond what is familiar and convenient.

3. I am learning from Setbacks: Setbacks and failures are not the end but stepping stones to progress. Both groups have shown us the importance of overcoming adversity, learning from mistakes, and using setbacks as opportunities for growth.

4. Mentorship Matters: The guidance and mentorship of experienced individuals play a pivotal role in one's journey to success. Seeking mentors' wisdom and insights can accelerate progress and help avoid costly mistakes.

5. Peak Performance: Pursuing peak performance is the zenith of achievement. It involves optimizing physical and mental capabilities and maintaining a relentless quest for excellence and continuous improvement.

6. Wealth and Well-Being: Striking a balance between financial success and personal well-being is essential. Both billionaires and bodybuilders emphasize the importance of maintaining health, relationships, and overall quality of life on the path to success.

Providing Actionable Advice for Readers to Apply in Their Own Lives

Success is not limited to the stories of the individuals we've explored but is a path anyone can embark upon.

Below, I want to provide you with some actionable advice that you can apply in your own life to help you achieve the success you're working towards.

1. Define Your Vision: Clarify your vision of success, considering personal and professional aspects. What does success mean to you, and what steps can you take to realize it?

2. Commit with Resolve: Success requires commitment. Commit to your goals and be prepared to work hard and overcome challenges.

3. Embrace Discomfort: Don't shy away from discomfort and challenges. Recognize that growth often comes from stepping outside your comfort zone.

4. Learn from Setbacks: When you encounter setbacks, see them as opportunities for growth. Analyze what went wrong, make necessary adjustments, and use setbacks as stepping stones to future success.

5. Seek Mentorship: Identify individuals who can offer guidance and mentorship in your chosen field. Learn from their experiences, seek their advice, and leverage their knowledge.

6. Pursue Peak Performance: Continuously strive to optimize your physical and mental capabilities. Set high standards for yourself and commit to a journey of continuous improvement.

7. Balance Wealth and Well-Being: Prioritize your well-being as you pursue success. Maintain a healthy balance between financial achievements and overall quality of life.

Inspiring and Motivating the Readers to Pursue Their Dreams

As we conclude our exploration of the lives of billionaires and bodybuilders, I hope their journeys have inspired and motivated you to pursue your dreams.

While each individual's path to success is unique, the principles of commitment, resilience, and unwavering determination remain constant.

Remember that success is not an exclusive domain reserved for the few; it is an open path anyone can tread. Use this book's lessons as a source of inspiration, guidance, and motivation as you embark on your own quest for success.

The stories of billionaires and bodybuilders throughout this book are testaments to the remarkable potential of the human spirit.

As you embark on your journey to success, embrace the commitment, determination, and resilience that define your paths.

With your vision clear, your resolve unwavering, and your determination undeterred, you, too, can write your own success story—one that is equal but uniquely yours.

Chapter 10 Key Takeaways

- Commitment is essential for success, as demonstrated by both billionaires and bodybuilders.

- Unyielding dedication helps you overcome challenges and achieve dreams.

- Growth occurs outside comfort zones, a lesson from both groups.

- Success often lies just beyond what is familiar and convenient.

- Setbacks are opportunities for growth, not endpoints.

- Overcoming adversity and learning from mistakes are crucial for progress.

- Seeking guidance from mentors accelerates progress and avoids mistakes.

- Pursuing peak performance involves optimizing physical and mental capabilities.

- Continuous improvement and a relentless quest for excellence are key.

- Balancing financial success with personal well-being is crucial.

- Maintaining health, relationships, and overall quality of life is important.

- Clarify personal and professional goals to define success.

- Hard work and commitment are necessary for success.

- Growth often comes from stepping outside comfort zones.

- Analyze setbacks, make adjustments, and use them as stepping stones.

- Gain guidance and advice from experienced mentors.

- Continuously strive for improvement in physical and mental capabilities.

- Prioritize overall well-being alongside financial achievements.

- Success is attainable by anyone willing to commit, persevere, and learn.

- Use the lessons from billionaires and bodybuilders as inspiration on your journey.

Final Thoughts

As we approach the conclusion of this book and our journey together, we find ourselves at a crossroads—a point of reflection, inspiration, and determination.

The pages we have explored have been a testament to the paths of billionaires and bodybuilders, their triumphs and tribulations, and the common threads that weave through their journeys toward success.

In this final section of the book, we will wrap up and reiterate the message that the road to success is equal for all who dare to take it and encourage readers to embark on their journeys.

You don't need to strive to be a billionaire or bodybuilder, but the lessons learned and key takeaways from this book will ring true no matter what you want to do with your life.

Wrapping Up the Book

Our journey through the lives of billionaires and bodybuilders has been an exploration of the diverse yet interwoven paths to success.

We have witnessed the unwavering commitment, resilience, and determination propel individuals toward their goals. We have dug deep into embracing discomfort, learning from setbacks, and optimizing one's capabilities for peak performance. We've uncovered the significance of mentorship and the delicate balance between wealth and well-being.

Reiterating the Message

The central message throughout these pages is that the road to success is equal and accessible to all who dare to take it. Commitment, resilience, and determination remain constants regardless of one's chosen domain or pursuits.

Success is not reserved for a select few but is an open path waiting to be ventured upon.

The stories of billionaires and bodybuilders testify to the human spirit's remarkable potential and what they can do.

They exemplify that success is not limited by circumstance, background, or occupation. It is a journey that anyone can embark upon, defined by their unique vision of success and the unwavering commitment to realizing that vision.

Maya Angelou said it best when he was quoted saying, "Nothing will work unless you do."

Nothing has ever been more accurate. If you're not willing to put in the work, do not expect to find success. Success comes with blood, sweat, and tears.

It's about getting your hands dirty, keeping your head in the clouds and hands in the dirt.

Never be afraid to dream, but never feel too scared to act.

The Time Has Come to Start Your Journey Toward Success

As we close this book, we invite you, our readers, to embark on your own journeys to success. Just as bodybuilders sculpt their bodies and billionaires shape their empires, you can mold your path to success.

Define your vision of success, commit with unwavering determination, embrace discomfort, and learn from setbacks. Seek mentorship and continually strive to optimize your physical and mental capabilities. Balance your pursuit of wealth with well-being, and remember that success is not a destination but a lifelong journey of continuous improvement.

The road to success is equal, but it is yours to traverse. As you start your journey, remember the lessons learned from the lives of billionaires and bodybuilders. Draw inspiration from their commitment and resilience, and let their stories be a source of guidance and motivation.

The pages of this book have provided a glimpse into the possibilities that await you. As you turn the page to begin your adventure, remember that success is not an endpoint but a lifelong pursuit. It is a path open to all who dare to take it, defined by your unique vision and unwavering commitment to chasing your dreams.

The journey is yours, and the road to success is equal for all. Now, go out there and win.

How to Stay in Touch with the Authors

As you turn the last page of this book, we want to express our heartfelt gratitude for your choice to read it. Your support means the world to us, and we hope the words within these pages have provided you with the blueprint to help you succeed in life.

Writing this book has been a labor of love and a culmination of countless hours of hanging out with and speaking to bodybuilders and those who have accumulated unimaginable wealth through entrepreneurship.

We've always said that bodybuilders make the best entrepreneurs, and hopefully, this book will help you understand how we came to this conclusion.

It has been a privilege to share our thoughts, stories, and ideas with you, and we sincerely hope they have resonated with you deeply and meaningfully.

Our connection and work don't have to end here. We would love to stay in touch and learn about how the pages in this book have helped you build the success you envisioned for yourself. You can follow us on social media, where we often share our thoughts, insights, and glimpses into our daily lives:

Matt Weik

Twitter: WeikFitness

Instagram: WeikFitness

Facebook: WeikFitnessLLC, WritingRebels, or my personal account, MattWeik.Fitness

LinkedIn: MattWeik

You can also stay in touch by visiting my websites, www.WeikFitness.com, www.TheWritingRebels.com, and www.MattWeik.com.

Feel free to subscribe to my weekly newsletter at WeikFitness.com, where you'll receive exclusive content, early access to my upcoming works, and the opportunity to discuss my works with fellow readers.

Marc Lobliner

Twitter: MarcLobliner

Instagram: MarcLobliner

Facebook: Lobliner

LinkedIn: MarcLobliner

YouTube: TigerFitness

You can also stay in touch by visiting my websites, MarcLobliner.com, TigerFitness.com, MTSnutrition.com, and AmbrosiaCollective.com.

We value your feedback and cherish the connections forged through our shared love of building muscle and wealth.

Your reviews, comments, and messages inspire us to continue creating, exploring, and pushing the boundaries.

Remember, this book is just one chapter in the ongoing narrative of our connection. We look forward to many more adventures together through the written word.

Thank you again for your support, and may your journey through life's pages be filled with joy, enlightenment, and endless wonder.

www.ingramcontent.com/pod-product-compliance
Lightning Source LLC
Chambersburg PA
CBHW061333120726
48001CB00002B/845